CONFESSIONS OF AN EX-MORMON

Recovery Journal

TRACY TENNANT

Right Track Publishing

Olathe, Kansas

Confessions of an Ex-Mormon Recovery Journal
From Kolob To Calvary Volume 2
Copyright © 2016 Tracy Tennant

All rights reserved. No part of this publication may be reproduced or transmitted in any form or by any means, including informational storage and retrieval systems, without permission in writing from the copyright holder, except for brief quotations in a review.

Right Track Publishing
P.O. Box 4712, Olathe, KS 66063
First Edition: February 2016
Printed in the United States of America
ISBN: 978-0-9913371-0-1

Cover photo courtesy of NASA
Cover and Interior Design and Layout by Tracy Tennant

*This journal is dedicated
to those whose lives have been turned upside down
for the sake of truth.*

Table of Contents

Introduction: Why Journal About Leaving Mormonism	1
Awakening: Journey Out	2
Relationships	15
Recovery: Positives and Negatives	34
Blunders, Bungles, and Better Strategies	53
Support	70
Serious Stuff	79
Fun Stuff	98
Action Steps	102
Fill in your own topic	105
Fill in your own topic	107
Six Months Later	109
One Year Later	121
Two Years and Beyond	131
Notes	141

Introduction

When you divulge your doubts about the church to others, especially if you make a declarative statement that you no longer believe it's true, chances are high that you'll be met with resistance, consternation, anger, or rejection. Keeping a journal thus becomes helpful--maybe even therapeutic--for several reasons.

First, it's a safe place to vent your feelings and frustrations. When you go through the experience of discovering that Mormonism isn't what it claims to be, the emotions are overwhelming. Life becomes difficult as you try to navigate out of the LDS worldview and into what you hope is reality. Writing in a journal is an outlet where you can express yourself openly, honestly, and without fear of reprisal.

Second, journaling your way out of Mormonism gives some perspective. You won't know how far you've come if you don't know where you've been. Reflecting on the challenges you faced and how you overcame them can encourage you to press on and give you a sense of accomplishment. Additionally, sharing your experiences with others who are seeking help leaving Mormonism behind could be cathartic for you, as well as for them.

Third, recording and documenting events, experiences, conversations, and interactions could be very useful if you become entangled in legal matters arising from your departure from the church. Sadly, divorces, custody battles, harassment, and other unpleasant situations are all too common when formerly devout Mormons "leave the fold."

Finally, this is YOUR LIFE! Being LDS and former LDS will always be a part of who you are. Learn from what you're going through. Grow from it. Don't let bitterness take root; it will only keep you from being truly alive.

Awakening

*"Ignorance is the curse of God;
knowledge is the wing wherewith we fly to heaven."*
~ William Shakespeare ~

I first began to question Mormonism when:

The events leading up to my decision to leave the church:

List of issues that trouble me the most about the church:

Doctrines and/or policies I don't feel comfortable with:

Questions I want answers to:

Who I went to in the church for answers:

Relationships

"A family is a risky venture because the greater the love, the greater the loss; that's the trade-off. But I'll take it all."

~ Brad Pitt ~

When I told my (spouse or parents) my doubts about the church, the reaction I got was:

_____
_____
_____
_____
_____
_____
_____
_____
_____
_____
_____
_____
_____

When I told my family (kids, siblings, in-laws) I didn't believe the church was true, they reacted by:

My closest friends reacted by:

When members of the ward found out I left, they:

"The most painful goodbyes are the ones never said and never explained."
— Unknown

Over all, my relationships with others have changed in these ways:

_____
_____
_____
_____
_____
_____
_____
_____
_____
_____
_____
_____
_____
_____
_____

Things that hurt me the most:

Rumors and untruths circulating about me and why I left the church:

"Gossip doesn't need to be false to be evil; there's a lot of truth that shouldn't be passed around."
Frank A. Clark

The Most Outrageous Things Mormons have said to me:

The Most Loving Thing an LDS Person Said to Me:

Who, What, When?

Who, What, When?

Who, What, When?

Recovery

"Recovery begins from the darkest moment."

~ John Major ~

The Negatives

What grieves me the most about my time spent as a Mormon:

My three biggest regrets are:

One

Two

Three

Things I won't miss about being LDS:

The callings I disliked the most and why:

Things that are harder than I expected after leaving Mormonism:

My biggest fears about leaving the church:

The Postives

Beneficial things I learned from being Mormon:

Things I liked about being Mormon:

My callings I liked the most and why:

**Things that are easier than I expected
after leaving the church::**

The best thing about leaving the church is:

Blunders, Bungles, & Better Strategies

"I have not failed. I've just found 10,000 ways that won't work."

~ Thomas Edison ~

Sometimes we don't handle things so well and wish we would have done it differently. These are some situations that fall in that category!

Situation

Blunder

Better

Situation

Blunder

Better

Situation

Blunder

Better

Situation

Blunder

Better

Situation

Blunder

Better

List some insensitive comments that LDS friends or relatives might make and how I will respond:

Example: The bishop says that I lost my testimony because of sin. My response will be, "Whether I've sinned or not, it doesn't change the fact that Joseph Smith took other men's wives."

Comment:

_____
_____
_____
_____

Response:

_____
_____
_____
_____

Comment:

Response:

Comment:

Response:

Comment:

Response:

Comment:

Response:

Comment:

Response:

Comment:

Response:

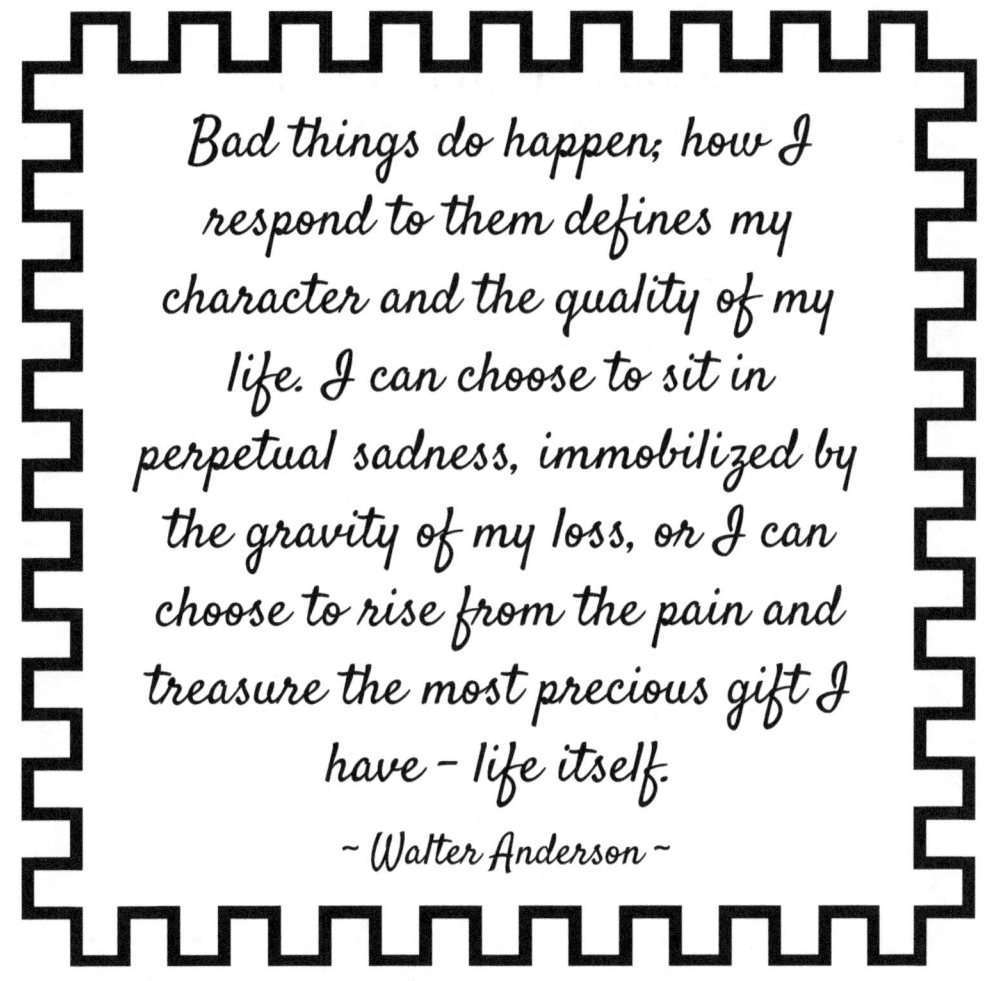

Bad things do happen; how I respond to them defines my character and the quality of my life. I can choose to sit in perpetual sadness, immobilized by the gravity of my loss, or I can choose to rise from the pain and treasure the most precious gift I have – life itself.

~ Walter Anderson ~

It's inevitable that people will hurt me, intentionally or unintentionally. I might be excluded from a family event, "un-friended" on social media, or in other ways rejected. Although it doesn't remove the sting, being prepared in advance can ameliorate some of the pain.

Responding to Hurtful Actions

What are some hurtful scenarios I can anticipate and how might I best respond?

Support

*"A real friend is one who walks in when
the rest of the world walks out"*

~ Walter Winchell ~

As I transitioned out of Mormonism, these are the individuals who stood by me or offered to help:

_____
_____
_____
_____
_____
_____
_____
_____
_____
_____
_____
_____
_____

Ex-LDS support groups I belong to or am thinking of joining locally or online:

Name
Link / Location
Contact

_____
_____
_____
_____

Name
Link / Location
Contact

_____
_____
_____
_____

Name
Link / Location
Contact

_____
_____
_____
_____

Name

Link / Location

Contact

Name

Link / Location

Contact

Name

Link / Location

Contact

Name

Link / Location

Contact

Websites, Books, and Videos

List of websites, books, videos, and podcasts that were most helpful as I researched Mormonism:

When I feel alone or down, I usually do these things to feel better (the good, the bad, and the ugly):

Keeping the previous things in mind, what else can I do that would help me take care of my emotional, relational, and spiritual needs:

Serious Stuff

"I am determined to be cheerful and happy in whatever situation I may find myself. For I have learned that the greater part of our misery or unhappiness is determined not by our circumstance, but by our disposition."

~ Martha Washington ~

Values I learned in Mormonism that I want to keep and the reasons why:

_____
_____
_____
_____
_____
_____
_____
_____
_____
_____
_____
_____

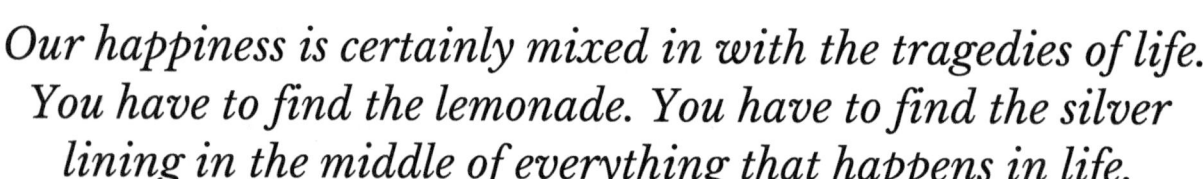

Our happiness is certainly mixed in with the tragedies of life. You have to find the lemonade. You have to find the silver lining in the middle of everything that happens in life.

~ Chandra Wilson ~

Views I held as a member of the church that I want to keep and why:

POLITICAL   RELIGIOUS   EDUCATIONAL

SOCIAL   LIFESTYLE

ETCETERA

_____
_____
_____
_____
_____
_____
_____
_____
_____
_____
_____
_____
_____
_____
_____
_____

Views and values I held as a Mormon that I want to abandon and why:

What am I willing to do to save my marriage or relationships with the Mormons in my life?

Deal  Breakers

What are deal breakers in my relationships with LDS? At what point do I "just say no?"

My thoughts about God and spiritual matters:

Fun Stuff

"Never, ever underestimate the importance of having fun."
~ Randy Pausch ~

☐ *I do* ☐ *I do not*

intend to drink coffee and tea because:

_____
_____
_____
_____

☐ *I do* ☐ *I do not*

intend to try alcoholic beverages because:

_____
_____
_____
_____

My First Coffee Adventure

What, where, and with whom?

_____
_____
_____
_____
_____
_____
_____

You can't buy happiness

but you can BUY COFFEE

And that's pretty close

Coffee drinks I've tried

- ☐ Black
- ☐ With cream
- ☐ Frappacino
- ☐ Latte
- ☐ Flavored
- ☐ Espresso
- ☐ Mocha
- ☐ Cappacino

Roasts

- ☐ Light
- ☐ Medium
- ☐ Dark
- ☐ Italian
- ☐ French

Notes:
_____
_____
_____
_____
_____
_____
_____

"God grant me coffee to change the things I can; Wine to accept the things I cannot, and a thermos so my Mormon family can't tell the difference."

Beer, Wine, and Spirits

Trading temple garments for "Funderwear"

Tell all about it! Did it feel strange?

What changes have I made to my wardrobe?
Did leaving the church affect the way I dress?

Things I look forward to as a non-Mormon:
Plans big and small:

Action Steps

Things I need to do for recovery and restoration:

Examples:
Write resignation letter, Tell family, Released from callings, Move...

- [ ] _____
- [ ] _____
- [ ] _____
- [ ] _____
- [ ] _____
- [ ] _____
- [ ] _____
- [ ] _____
- [ ] _____
- [ ] _____
- [ ] _____
- [ ] _____

Issues I want to address in my resignation letter:

Six Months

Six months after leaving the church, what things have changed? What has remained the same? Are things better or worse? How so?

One Year

One year after leaving the church, what things have changed? How am I different? How are my relationships?

Two Years & Beyond

How life has changed:

Notes